The Seeds of the Milkweed

By Mrs. Hicks
Second Grade Class
East End Elementary
Little Rock, Arkansas

Scholastic Inc.   New York   Toronto   London   Auckland   Sydney   Mexico City   New Delhi   Hong Kong   Buenos Aires

We dedicate this book
to our families,
teachers and staff of
East End Elementary,
to the Monarch Butterflies,
and to everybody who
loves and appreciates
beautiful creatures.

These are the seeds of the milkweed.

This is the soil in the flower pot, shiny and red,
Where we planted the seeds of the milkweed
So they will be fed.

This is the watering can, orange and mellow,
Used to water the soil in the flower pot, shiny and red,
Where we planted the seeds of the milkweed
So they will be fed.

This is the sun, round and yellow.

And the watering can, orange and mellow,
Used to water the soil in the flower pot, shiny and red,
Where we planted the seeds of the milkweed
So they will be fed.

This is a sprout, green and small.

Warmed by the sun, round and yellow,
Drinking from the watering can, orange and mellow,
Growing in the soil in the flower pot, shiny and red,
Where we planted the seeds of the milkweed
So they will be fed.

This is the sky, vast and tall.

Providing room for the sprout, green and small,
Warmed by the sun, round and yellow,
Drinking from the watering can, orange and mellow,
Growing in the soil in the flower pot, shiny and red,
Where we planted the seeds of the milkweed
So they will be fed.

These are the brightly colored purple blooms.

Reaching to the blue sky, vast and tall,
Providing room for the sprout, green and small,
Warmed by the sun, round and yellow,
Drinking from the watering can, orange and mellow,
Growing in the soil in the flower pot, shiny and red,
Where we planted the seeds of the milkweed
So they will be fed.

This is the adult Monarch, dressed in a black, white and orange costume.

Attracted to the brightly colored purple blooms,
Reaching to the blue sky, vast and tall,
Providing room for the sprout, green and small,
Warmed by the sun, round and yellow,
Drinking from the watering can, orange and mellow,
Growing in the soil in the flower pot, shiny and red,
Where we planted the seeds of the milkweed
So they will be fed.

These are the miniature white eggs,
laid under the leaves-es.

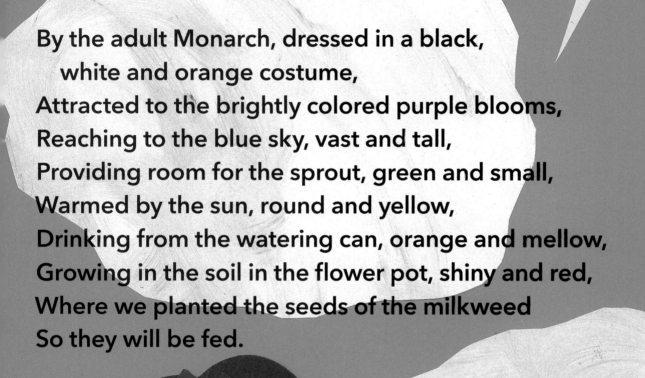

By the adult Monarch, dressed in a black,
  white and orange costume,
Attracted to the brightly colored purple blooms,
Reaching to the blue sky, vast and tall,
Providing room for the sprout, green and small,
Warmed by the sun, round and yellow,
Drinking from the watering can, orange and mellow,
Growing in the soil in the flower pot, shiny and red,
Where we planted the seeds of the milkweed
So they will be fed.

This is the munch-munching caterpillar, that eats as it pleases.

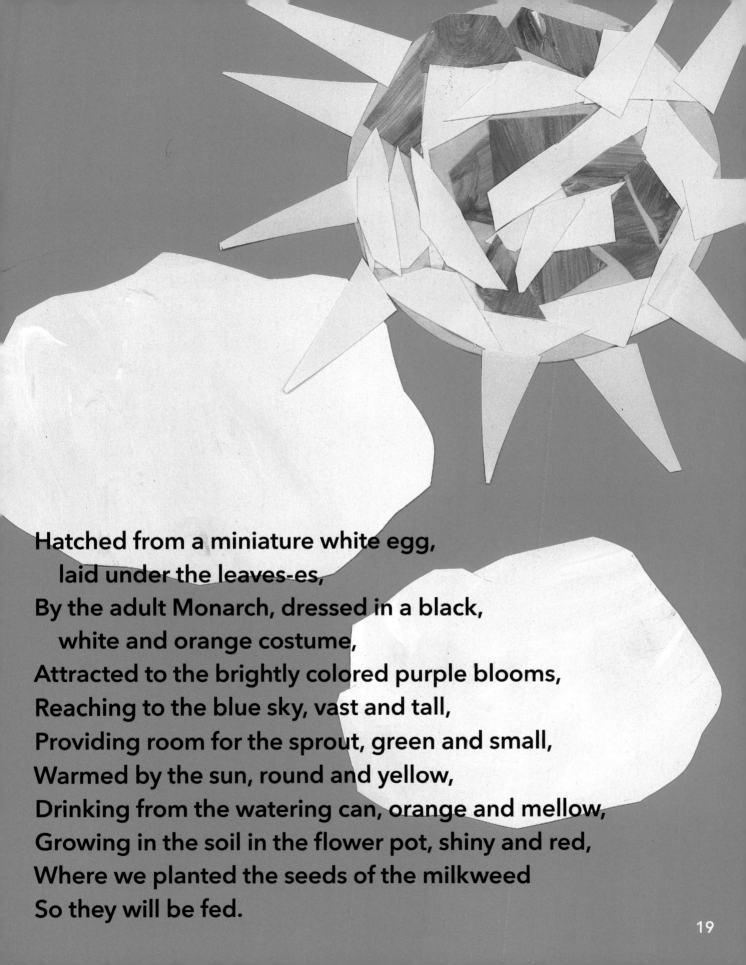

Hatched from a miniature white egg,
 laid under the leaves-es,
By the adult Monarch, dressed in a black,
 white and orange costume,
Attracted to the brightly colored purple blooms,
Reaching to the blue sky, vast and tall,
Providing room for the sprout, green and small,
Warmed by the sun, round and yellow,
Drinking from the watering can, orange and mellow,
Growing in the soil in the flower pot, shiny and red,
Where we planted the seeds of the milkweed
So they will be fed.

This is the chubby larva,
hanging upside down.

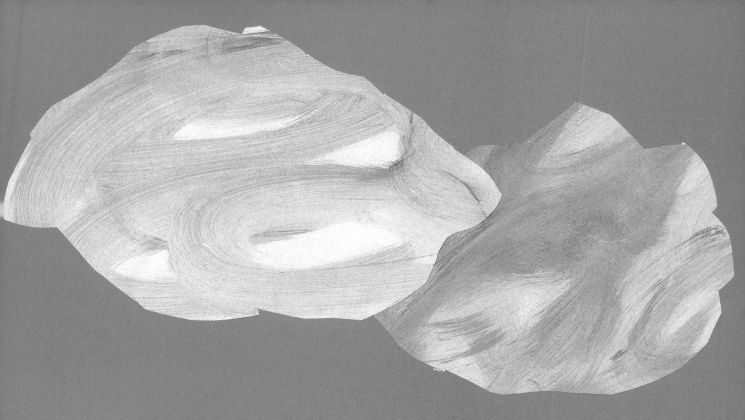

Who started as a munch-munching caterpillar,
    that eats as it pleases,
Hatched from a miniature white egg,
    laid under the leaves-es,
By the adult Monarch, dressed in a black,
    white and orange costume,
Attracted to the brightly colored purple blooms,
Reaching to the blue sky, vast and tall,
Providing room for the sprout, green and small,
Warmed by the sun, round and yellow,
Drinking from the watering can, orange and mellow,
Growing in the soil in the flower pot, shiny and red,
Where we planted the seeds of the milkweed
So they will be fed.

This is an extraordinary pupa,
decorated with a golden crown.

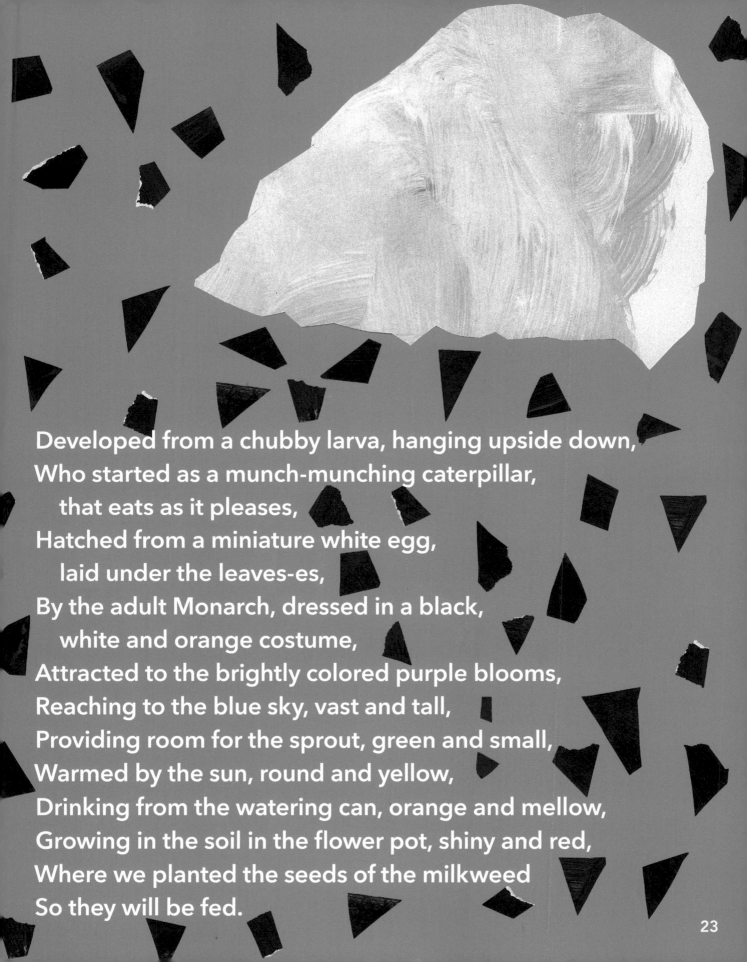

Developed from a chubby larva, hanging upside down,
Who started as a munch-munching caterpillar,
 that eats as it pleases,
Hatched from a miniature white egg,
 laid under the leaves-es,
By the adult Monarch, dressed in a black,
 white and orange costume,
Attracted to the brightly colored purple blooms,
Reaching to the blue sky, vast and tall,
Providing room for the sprout, green and small,
Warmed by the sun, round and yellow,
Drinking from the watering can, orange and mellow,
Growing in the soil in the flower pot, shiny and red,
Where we planted the seeds of the milkweed
So they will be fed.

This is the adult, metamorphosis complete.

Emerging from the extraordinary pupa,
   decorated with a golden crown,
Developed from a chubby larva,
   hanging upside down,
Who started as a munch-munching caterpillar,
   that eats as it pleases,
Hatched from a miniature white egg,
   laid under the leaves-es,
By the adult Monarch, dressed in a black,
   white and orange costume,
Attracted to the brightly colored purple blooms,
Reaching to the blue sky, vast and tall,
Providing room for the sprout, green and small,
Warmed by the sun, round and yellow,
Drinking from the watering can, orange and mellow,
Growing in the soil in the flower pot, shiny and red,
Where we planted the seeds of the milkweed
So they will be fed.

This is the milkweed, with flowers so sweet.

Feeding the adult, metamorphosis complete,
Emerging from the extraordinary pupa,
   decorated with a golden crown,
Developed from a chubby larva, hanging upside down,
Who started as a munch-munching caterpillar,
   that eats as it pleases,
Hatched from a miniature white egg, laid under the leaves-es,
By the adult Monarch, dressed in a black,
   white and orange costume,
Attracted to the brightly colored purple blooms,
Reaching to the blue sky, vast and tall,
Providing room for the sprout, green and small,
Warmed by the sun, round and yellow,
Drinking from the watering can, orange and mellow,
Growing in the soil in the flower pot, shiny and red,
Where we planted the seeds of the milkweed
So they will be fed.

MEET THE AUTHORS

Top, left to right: Enzo Henry, Casey Vang, Gabby Villanueva, Emma Henard, Xander Dalton, Nate Nantharangsy, Alyssa Keary, John Eckert

Middle, left to right: James Peel, Kylie Witty, Kirsten Milam, Patrick Gentry, Alivia Reeves, Jackson Dowler, Madison Tippins, Brycen Dobbins

Front, left to right: Jessie Smotherman, Alexis Stephens, Kaley Osborne, Harley Wagner, Christian Miranda, Kyler Burke, Emily Freeman, Zoë Bryant, Arlee Ward

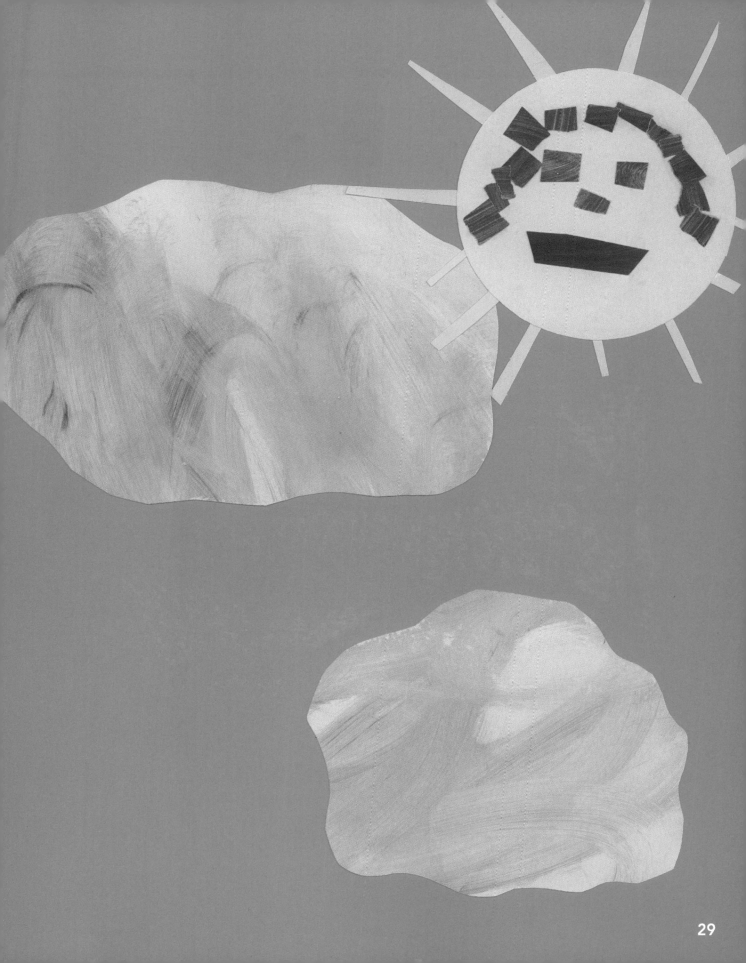

Kids Are Authors®
Books written by children for children

The Kids Are Authors® Competition was established in 1986 to encourage
children to read and to become involved in the creative process of writing.
Since then, thousands of children have written and illustrated books as participants
in the Kids Are Authors® Competition.

The winning books in the annual competition are published by Scholastic Inc.
and are distributed by Scholastic Book Fairs throughout the United States.

For more information:
Kids Are Authors® 1080 Greenwood Blvd., Lake Mary, FL 32746
Or visit our website at: www.scholastic.com/kidsareauthors

For information regarding permission, write to Scholastic Inc.,
Attention: Permission Department, 557 Broadway, New York, NY 10012.

ISBN-978-0-545-64593-5
12 11 10 9 8 7 6 5 4 3 2 1

Cover design by Bill Henderson
Printed and bound in the U.S.A.
First Printing, June 2013